SATB

S0-BNJ-161

Come Walk With Me

Through the Passion and Resurrection of Christ

Pepper Choplin

Instrumentation by Stan Pethel

Editor: Larry F. Pugh
Music Engraving: Linda Taylor
Cover Design: Jeff Richards

ISBN: 978-1-4291-2293-1

Lorenz

A Lorenz Company • www.lorenz.com

Sacred Music for Sacred Moments... from the composer

Throughout the writing process, I was striving to compose sacred music— music that conveyed these profoundly sacred moments in Jesus' life. I tried to carefully craft the music to convey the hushed voices and soft light of His last Passover meal, the tension and anguish of Gethsemane, and the paradox and power of the cross.

The narration style was inspired by the PBS documentaries of Ken Burns. I visualize the readings being done from offstage, perhaps with some visuals on a screen. Feel free to adapt the material to your own situation. Have the readers speak the passages with an unhurried pace. The words should not be emotionalized, but read as an engaging lecture. The character quotes should be read in a subdued, intimate style as if reading a quote from a diary. Speak the names at the end of each as an audible signing of the passage. The narrator should simply lead the listener through the story. The music supplies the drama and the passion.

Come Walk With Me—In each version of this song, the soloist and the choir should try to draw the listeners in—to lead them to see and feel the drama of the story. The first solo could be sung from the congregation while walking toward the front.

Blessed Is He Who Comes—"Feel the moment" as the soloist signals the distant arrival of Christ. Then the choir bursts into joyful celebration and praise. The style of the music is not meant to be frivolous, but a fresh way to express the exuberance of the moment.

The Upper Room—I was really feeling the "soft and flickering light" of the scene here. It was such an intimate setting in which Jesus said goodbye. Later, the piece breaks out of the intimacy and rushes through the passage, "go quickly now and do what you must do." Then it settles into resignation as it repeats, "go do what you must do."

Crossroads at Gethsemane—Feel the inner turmoil and tension of Christ's decision. Later, allow the music to explode into the text, "Look, the betrayer is at hand." Be especially careful with the final consonants through this piece. On the final measure, experiment to find the right effect for the four beats of the soft, sustaining "ssssss."

Hanging on a Cross—Notice the constant change of major and minor throughout. This is to convey the paradox of the prophet and healer being hung on a cross. Accentuate the contrast of the major and minor harmonic phrases. Sing the beginning of each verse more brightly. Then add weight to the phrase, "He's hanging on a cross."

Lay His Body Down—Notice the descending melodies as the body is "lowered down." Sing with a clean, straight tone to allow the different parts to be heard. Perhaps, control the higher sections a bit and add fullness to the lower range. Add a little muscle for the climax with the high E's in part one. Strive for a bell-shaped level of intensity as the music builds to its climax, then tapers to the end.

No Greater Love—After all the tension and pain, this song is meant to be a relief—a time of sweet reflection on the extraordinary meaning and significance of the cross. The piano should imitate a guitar with smooth, precise articulations. Feel the steadiness of the beat.

He Arose—You may choose to save this piece for your Easter service. If so, the work will end naturally with *No Greater Love*, followed by the choral benediction.

Come Walk With Me Into the World—In this benediction, you may choose to have the soloist slowly walk toward the back of the sanctuary while singing of "going into the world."

—Pepper Choplin

Companion Products

55/1149L	SAB Score
55/1150L	SATB Score with CD
30/2663L	Orchestral Score and Parts
	Fl, Ob, Eng Hn, Penny Whistle, 2 Tpt, 2 Tbn, Dulcimer, Autoharp,
	Gtr, Banjo, opt. Mandolin, 2 Perc, Timp, Pno, 2 Vln, Vla, Cello, Bass
30/2674L	Instrumental Ensemble Score and Parts
	Fl/Penny Whistle, Ob, Dulcimer, Autoharp, Gtr/Banjo, Pno,
	Digital Strings
99/2815L	Bulk Performance CDs (10 pak)
99/2816L	Accompaniment CD
99/2817L	SA/TB Part-dominant Rehearsal CDs (reproducible)

Lorenz is happy to provide to you downloadable images/graphics to help enhance your presentation of this work. These images are royalty-free, which means that you can use them for free promotional items like bulletins, posters, and fliers. We do request that you only use these for promotion of a live performance of a Lorenz piece.

To access these files, please visit www.lorenz.com/downloads and navigate to the desired folder. PC users should right click and choose "Save Target As..." and Macintosh users should click and hold the link, then choose "Save Target As..." We have provided standard file formats that should be usable in most page layout or word processing software.

If you are having difficulties, we suggest using the help feature of your particular software concerning images. Due to the vast number of differences in computer system setups, we are unable to provide technical support for downloadable images/graphics by either phone or email.

Contents

Come Walk With Me

Prologue

Music by
Pepper Choplin

Narrator: He was already thirty years old when He set out on His ministry. *(begin music)*
The name *Jesus* was a common one at the time.

People in His remote hometown didn't see Him as a great preacher or anything *else* very special. In fact, they ran Him out of town the first time He returned home.

To some, He was seen as a prophet; to others, a miracle worker and healer. To the religious establishment of the day, He was a challenge to their authority.

www.lorenz.com LT

Then, as His popularity grew, there was talk of Him being the promised Messiah, even the Son of God.

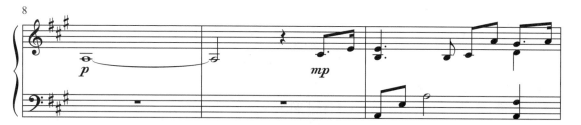

He traveled the countryside with twelve main disciples, though others followed close behind. He would preach His truths to one person face to face or to five thousand on a hillside.

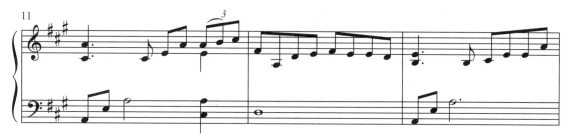

Woven into His teachings, there came more and more talk about His own death, first in shrouded terms, then ever more clearly.

For centuries, a prophet who was *anybody* was bound to end up in the holy city, Jerusalem. The road to Jerusalem drew Jesus like a magnet. *(music ends)*

Voice of Jesus: *(without music)* I will drive out demons and heal people today and tomorrow, and on the third day, I will reach my goal. In any case, I must keep going today and tomorrow and the next day—for surely, no *prophet* can die outside Jerusalem. *(slight pause)* Jesus of Nazareth.

8

Come Walk With Me

(choir stands after "Jesus of Nazareth" is spoken)

Words and Music by
Pepper Choplin

Lord.

Come and see where Je - sus

stood, hear the lies and scorn that He en -

dured.

Here, the trial where Je - sus was con -

demned. This is the place where the suf - f'ring would be -

gin. We'll fol - low Je - sus' foot-steps up the

hill, where He would fall be - neath the

14

cross. But for Je - sus, there would be no rest; they forced Him on to meet His death. Come walk with

⑦ mf   rit.   mp

55/1148L-14

15

me to this curs - ed place, see___ the

rough_____ and splin-tered___ cross_____ where the

Son of God was cru - ci - fied. Walk___ with me, see___ the

place where Je - sus died.

Walk with me this ho - ly

road. Come walk with me.

Narrator: He had walked the countryside for three years, preaching and teaching and performing miracles. Eyewitnesses reported Him giving sight to the blind and cleansing people who suffered from leprosy, the dreaded disease of the skin. The closer Jesus of Nazareth came to Jerusalem, the more His fame and following grew. By the time He reached the city's gates, a huge throng followed as residents of the city went out to meet Him.

Voice of Luke: When He came near the place where the road goes down to the Mount of Olives, the whole crowd of disciples began joyfully to praise God in loud voices for all the miracles they had seen: "Blessed is the King who comes in the name of the Lord! Peace in heaven and glory in the highest!"

Some of the Pharisees in the crowd said to Jesus, "Teacher, rebuke your disciples!" "I tell you," He replied, "if they keep quiet, the stones will cry out…" *(begin music)* Luke, the physician.

Blessed Is He Who Comes

Words and Music by
Pepper Choplin

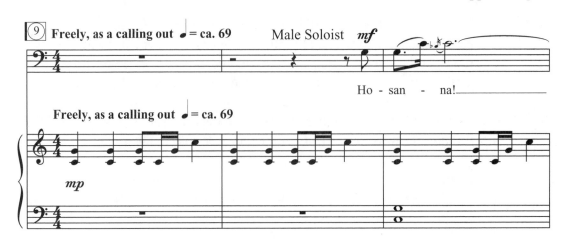

san - na! Bless-ed is He__ Who comes in the name of the__

rit.

10 **With underlying excitement** ♩ = ca. 92

Lord.

With underlying excitement ♩ = ca. 92

f

SA
mf

Rid - ing in__ pro - ces - sion, Je - sus came__ to town.

Peo - ple brought__ their coats__ and laid them on__ the

22

san - na,_____ ho - san - na!_____

Bless-ed is He____ Who comes in the name of the

Lord._____

⑬

SA
mf

Watch - ing in the crowd, there, were the Phar - i -

sees. When the peo - ple praised Him,

they were so dis - pleased.

TB
mf

Phar - i - sees said to Him, "Tell them not to

Bless-ed is He Who comes in the name of the Lord.

Ho - san - na, ho - san - na!

Bless-ed is He Who comes in the name of the

Lord."

Come now and save___ us, ho - ly Prom - ised One. The age of Mes - si - ah sure - ly has___ be -

Ho - san - na,_____ ho - san - na!_____

Bless-ed is He___ Who comes in the name of the

Lord."_____

Bless-ed is He___ who

*Optional solo.

Narrator: It was Passover in the city and thousands had turned up to celebrate the holy day in the *holiest* of cities. *(begin music)* Jesus directed two of His disciples to prepare for the Passover meal.

Come Walk With Me to the Upper Room

Solo

Words and Music by
Pepper Choplin

with Ped.

Voice of Peter: Jesus told John and me to go meet a man carrying a jar of water and say to him, "The Teacher asks you, 'Where is the guest room where I may eat the Passover with

My disciples?'" He showed us a large room upstairs in his house. There, as the Master had directed, we prepared the Passover meal. *(slight pause)* Simon Peter of Galilee.

Come walk with me to the up-per

32

The Upper Room

Words and Music by
Pepper Choplin

Come walk with me, I'll take you there, come soft-ly, fol-low up the stairs. The

34

55/1148L-34

29
28
rit.
mp
The
mp
The
rit.
32
Unhurried ♩ = ca. 58
ho - ly meal comes to an end,
the day of pain will
mp
ho - ly meal,
the day of pain,
Unhurried ♩ = ca. 58
34
mf
soon be - gin.
Be - fore they go, they sing a hymn
mp
mf
mf

and leave the up - per room.

When - ev - er now we come to share

the bread and cup that we pre - pare, re -

mem - ber all that hap - pened there_____ with - in the up - per

room, with - in the up - per room._____

(mm)

40

Narrator: After the Passover meal, Jesus took a few of His disciples with Him to the garden of Gethsemane. For Jesus, this was the crossroads of His life and ministry, both figuratively and literally. Gethsemane was located at the edge of Jerusalem. He could return to the city where leaders plotted against His life or leave Jerusalem and return to the freedom and fame He had experienced in the countryside. *(begin music)* The decision was a matter of life and death, and Jesus struggled intensely as He prayed.

Voice of Jesus: "Abba, Father, everything is possible for You. Take this cup from Me. *(slight pause)* Yet not *My* will, but *Yours* be done."

Crossroads at Gethsemane

Words and Music by
Pepper Choplin

LT

42

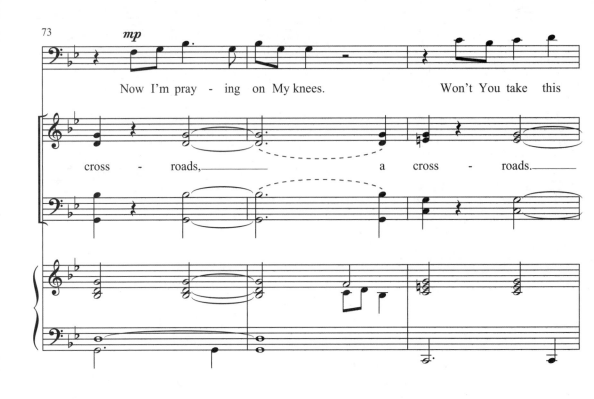

Now I'm pray - ing on My knees. Won't You take this

cross - roads,_____ a cross - roads._____

cup from Me? O— Ab - ba, Fa-ther, hear My prayer.

_____ Ab - ba, Fa-ther,_____ hear My

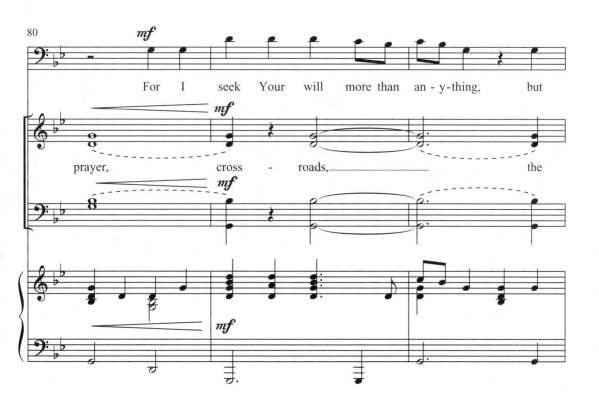

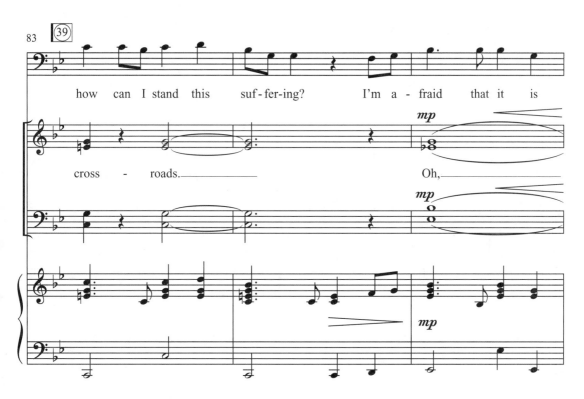

50

55/1148L-50

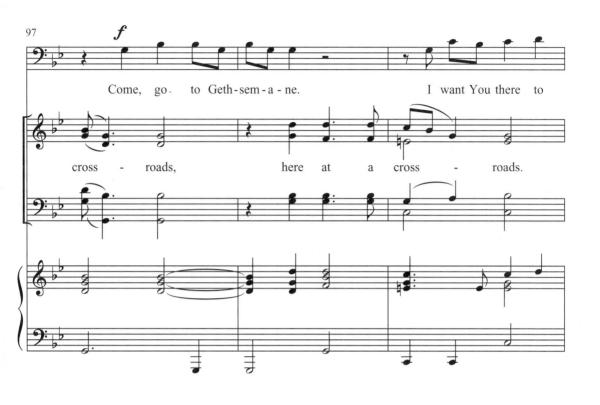

Come, go to Geth-sem-a-ne. I want You there to

cross - roads, here at a cross - roads.

pray with Me. Wait here and stay a-wake,

We're at a cross - roads, here at a

Wake up and rise! We stand at a cross-roads.

Here at a cross-roads,____ there's a road that

leads____ to a cross. We're on a road that

Come Walk With Me to the Cross

Words and Music by
Pepper Choplin

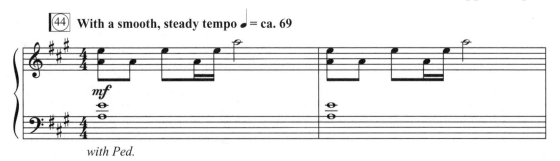

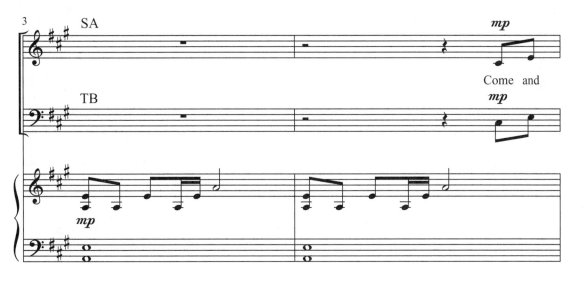

Je - sus' foot-steps up the hill, where He would

fall_____ be - neath the cross. But for

Je - sus, there would be no rest; they forced Him

on to meet His death.

Come walk with me to this curs - ed

place, see__ the rough_____ and splin-tered

cross_____ where the Son of God was cru - ci -

fied. Walk____ with me, see____ the place where He would

die._____ *(choir may be seated)*

*Accompaniment CD holds for 6 counts.

Narrator: The road to the cross would lead *first* to the high priests and the Sanhedrin, the seat of religious power in Jerusalem. After hours of interrogation, full of verbal and physical abuse, they were determined to have Him put to death. To do so, they would need to convince the seat of Roman law that Jesus was a threat to the government. They took Him to Pontius Pilate, the Roman governor. Pilate hardly wanted to become entangled in a fray on Jewish doctrine. However, he agreed to listen to the charges against Jesus.

Voice of Pontius Pilate: I gave this man, this Jesus of Nazareth, every opportunity to demonstrate His innocence. Instead, He hardly spoke, neither preaching nor defending Himself against the trumped-up charges. The Man was clearly innocent, and I tried just to have Him punished and released. This caused an uproar, and I was getting nowhere. So, to quiet the crowd, I washed my hands of the whole affair and handed Him over to be crucified. What is one man's life for the price of peace and quiet? *(slight pause)* Pontius Pilate.

Narrator: Before Jesus was taken to be crucified, Pilate had Him flogged. Then, to add a little theatrical flair for the crowd, the soldiers put a crown of thorns and a purple robe on Him. Some were amused; some were aghast; but many were simply curious to witness the spectacle of this execution. Those closest to Jesus were devastated.

Voice of John: I have never felt more sadness than at that moment at the cross. The sight of His tortured body, the blood, the wails of the women, and the shock and desperation on His mother's face will never leave my memory. The tears of His mother were almost more than I could bear. *(slight pause)* John, son of Zebedee.

Narrator: Followers of Jesus looked on in bewilderment. Some had left everything to follow this Man from Nazareth. They had seen Him perform miracles and thought He had come to Jerusalem to establish a new kingdom. Now, they watched in disbelief as the One they called Lord was taken and nailed to a cross. *(pause)*

Hanging on a Cross

(choir stands after "John, son of Zebedee" is spoken)

**Words and Music by
Pepper Choplin**

www.lorenz.com

LT

He placed His hands on a blind man, 'til the dark - ness left his eyes.

He healed the skin of the lep - ers when

He spoke of new life in hea - ven as if hea - ven was His home.

He preached the ho - ly word of God as if the

Word_____ was His own.

He spoke of love and sac - ri - fice and

what that love could cost. Now He's

cheered Him in - to town. They waved the palms be -

fore— Him and laid their gar - ments down. They

hailed Him as the Mes - si - ah as they

72

Narrator: *(begin music)* Though men were known to suffer for days before dying on a cross, it took a mere six hours before Jesus started to falter. After saying goodbye to His mother, He let out a loud groan...and died.

Voice of Jesus: Father, into Your hands I commit My Spirit.

Come Walk With Me, He Is Gone

Solo

Words and Music by
Pepper Choplin

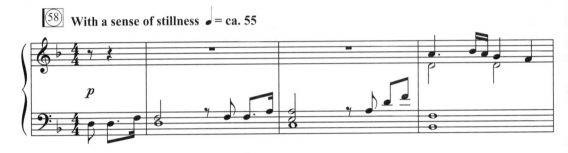

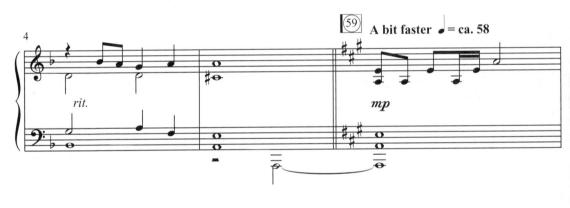

still, now His soul_____ is in God's

hands. When the spear is thrust in - to His

side, it____ is clear He____ is gone, the Lord has

died.

Lay His Body Down

Words by **Pepper Choplin**

Music by **William Billings**
"By the Waters of Babylon"
Arranged by **Pepper Choplin**

Si - lent - ly, so si - lent - ly, His bod - y hangs up - on the cross. Come re - move the nails, the

*The composer prefers that the choir be divided into three equal parts, with each part including both men and women. An alternate possibility would have Sopranos singing Part I, Altos on Part II, and all the men singing Part III.

78

55/1148L-78

No Greater Love

Words by **Isaac Watts**, alt.
and **Pepper Choplin**

Music by
Pepper Choplin

When I sur-vey___ the won-drous cross___

on which the Prince of Glo - ry___ died,

sor - row and love flow min - gled down.

Did e'er such love_____ and sor - row meet,_____

or thorns com - pose so rich_____ a

lyrics: to Your ex-am-ple, Your self-less love that nev-er ends? Were the whole realm

Narrator: The miraculous road for Jesus appeared to have ended. A few days earlier, He seemed to be on the brink of a glorious destiny. Now, His life had been violently cut short. His followers scattered, and His disciples went into hiding, fearing for their lives. One of them even committed suicide.

Just before sundown, the body of Jesus was taken down from the cross. Sabbath, the Jewish day of rest, was about to begin, so His body was hurriedly taken to a tomb borrowed from a sympathetic follower. According to Jewish law, no work was to be done during the Sabbath day, and so there was not time to prepare the body for burial. *(short pause)*

Early on the first morning after Sabbath, two of Jesus' friends, Mary Magdalene and Mary, the mother of James, started out to the grave with spices and perfumes with which they would anoint the body. *(begin music)* As they approached the tomb, they saw something that would change their lives and the lives of millions of people for generations.

Come Walk With Me to the Tomb

Soprano Solo

Words and Music by
Pepper Choplin

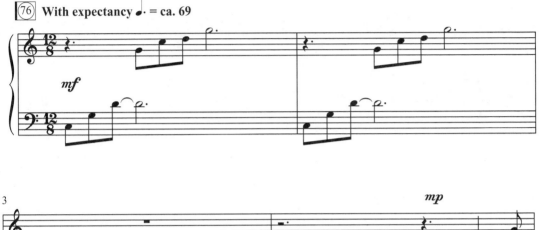

LT

warmth of the morn - ing sun. See the

stone,____ the stone is rolled a - way. Come__with me now__ to

hear the an - gel say: *(choir stands)*

He Arose

Words and Music by **Pepper Choplin**
Quoting CHRIST AROSE
by **Robert Lowry**, 1874

Why do you seek the liv-ing_____ here with the dead? Just as He said, He a-

rose._____ Why do you seek___ the liv-ing_____

104

Come Walk With Me Into the World
Benediction

Words and Music by
Pepper Choplin

Narrator: Lord, thank You for the story of Your sacrifice and love. Write it deep upon our hearts so that we will embody its Spirit and witness to its saving grace. Send us out now with the power of Your name in which we pray…